The Story of a
Mango Tree

written by
JEEVANA MIDTURI

Copyright © 2014 Jeevana Midturi

All rights reserved. No part of this book may be used or reproduced by any means, graphic, electronic, or mechanical, including photocopying, recording, taping or by any information storage retrieval system without the written permission of the publisher except in the case of brief quotations embodied in critical articles and reviews.

Inspiring Voices books may be ordered through booksellers or by contacting:

Inspiring Voices
1663 Liberty Drive
Bloomington, IN 47403
www.inspiringvoices.com
1 (866) 697-5313

Because of the dynamic nature of the Internet, any web addresses or links contained in this book may have changed since publication and may no longer be valid. The views expressed in this work are solely those of the author and do not necessarily reflect the views of the publisher, and the publisher hereby disclaims any responsibility for them.

Any people depicted in stock imagery provided by Thinkstock are models, and such images are being used for illustrative purposes only.
Certain stock imagery © Thinkstock.

ISBN: 978-1-4624-1070-5 (sc)
ISBN: 978-1-4624-1071-2 (e)

Printed in the United States of America.

Inspiring Voices rev. date: 1/14/2015

Inspiring Voices®

Dedicated.

To my grandchildren

Diya, Devan, Karis, and Stephen.

Dear all children, I am a mango tree and I wanted to tell you a bed time story. My beginning was from a seed. I sprouted as a tiny plant from the seed in a dust bin.

One day a little boy spotted me and picked me up and thought to himself, if I plant this plant in my garden it will grow big and it will give fruit to many people.

He planted me in his garden where there was enough water and good soil to grow.

I grew up experiencing summer, fall, winter, and spring.

On a beautiful day in one of the spring seasons, I started blooming and made many friends with bees, birds, animals and people. Bees came buzzing around me, birds sat on my branches to sing songs of beautiful melodies.

Birds built their nests on my limbs to lay their eggs. When winds blew and rains came, I spread my leaves around the nest and protected eggs from falling on the ground.

When chicks hatched, it was a happy sight. I watched chicks opening their mouths for food and mothers feeding tiny bits of food in chick's mouths and raising chicks to grow big. By now I have seen more than fifty generations of birds growing on me, and I wish to see many more in the future.

Animals like rabbits, squirrels, cats and dogs come under my tree to look for food. People sit under my shade to relax, take small naps under cool breeze. Some talk about their problems and enjoy company. I am only a tree but I will listen to their conversations.

When my flowers grew big and they turned in to green mangoes to begin with. In early summer green mangoes ripen in to golden yellow fruit with sweet aroma.

Birds, bees, animals, and people wait and watch every day for the ripened fruit. Birds are the first to spot the ripe fruit to peck and eat.

People pick the fruit and eat happily sitting under my shade. Some fill baskets with fruit, and take home and share with family and friends.

On the other day, I saw the boy who planted me. Now he grew big. He often comes to the garden to see me with his wife.

His wife hugs me and kisses me and I am delighted to see them both. I always smile at them and bless them to be prosperous, happy, and fruitful.

Dear children plant trees, eat fruits, be happy and healthy. Sweet dreams and goodnight.

ABOUT THE AUTHOR

Jeevana Midturi is a Teacher. She likes reading books and writing, gardening, knitting, tatting, and other hands on activities.

CPSIA information can be obtained at www.ICGtesting.com
Printed in the USA
LVOW05s1430070415

433617LV00035B/172/P